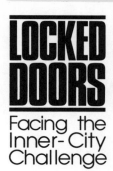

LOCKED DOORS

Facing the Inner-City Challenge

David A. Dolin

LOCKED DOORS

Facing the Inner-City Challenge

REGULAR BAPTIST PRESS
1300 North Meacham Road
Schaumburg, Illinois 60173-4888

Library of Congress Cataloging-in-Publication Data

Dolin, David A., 1939–
    Locked doors.

    1. Evangelistic work—Ohio—Cleveland.   2. Dolin, David A.,
1939–   .   3. Crime and criminals—Ohio—Cleveland. I. Title.
BV3775.C58D65   1989   253'.09173'2   89-8381
ISBN 0–87227–129–3

© 1989
Regular Baptist Press
Schaumburg, Illinois 60173-4888

Dedication: To my wife Marilyn, who shared these and many other experiences with me. She has proved herself to be a dedicated, supportive and loving helpmeet.

Contents

Foreword

You are about to read an interesting, exciting and factual book. The Rev. David A. Dolin has done an excellent job. With him, you will walk as I did through the fascinating but dangerous heart of a major city. At times, you will be chilled by the confrontation, by threatened harm and possible death. At other points, you will share the torment, the sadness and the crushing sense of futility that presses upon the people in the concrete canyons of the city.

Your eyes are soon to focus upon a sequence of sights they may be seeing for the first time. Your emotions will sense the impact of situations that produce all the feelings of which you are capable. You will not escape the sorrow, the fear, the loneliness, the hope, the happiness or the relief that rise like mists from the pavement and engulf the population of the inner city.

You are about to become friends with an amazing dog—and you had better become his friend! You will find it easier to walk the streets and alleys, to climb the dark stairways and to enter the forbidding official buildings of the big city as you feel this magnificent animal pulling on the leash in your hand. Admitting that you feel better because the dog is there, you may also recognize with David

Dolin that your steps are guarded by a much greater source of assurance.

You will, if you agree, enjoy the venture of walking with Christ along the way and into the homes and the hearts of the city. You will love the people if you will yield to the example of the love He has for them. You will sense the meaning of salvation as you watch people placing their personal faith in the Lord Jesus Christ. You will also gain a fresh understanding of what it means to die unsaved as you watch those city-dwellers who reject Christ for alcohol, drugs and the other snares of Satan that trap and destroy them.

Adventure and opportunity are in your hands. Perhaps as you proceed in company with David Dolin, you will encounter your *own* need for Christ, your *personal* surrender to His lordship or even your recognition that He wants you to serve Him in the inner city— or somewhere.

C. Raymond Buck, Ph.D.
President, Baptist Mid-Missions
Cleveland, Ohio

Introduction

The city is an interesting place. Most of those who read this book will be shocked by the experiences of this veteran missionary to needy people. The city is a mission field often overlooked by "mission-minded" churches in the same community. For some reason, Christians have failed to recognize "fields that are white unto harvest" located just a few miles from the comfortable pews of their lovely suburban churches.

Job's discourse, in one place, focused on the city. He said, "Men groan from out of the city, and the soul of the wounded crieth out. . . . They are of those that rebel against the light; they know not the ways thereof, nor abide in the paths thereof. The murderer rising with the light killeth the poor and needy, and in the night is as a thief. The eye also of the adulterer waiteth for the twilight, saying, No eye shall see me: and disguiseth his face. In the dark they dig through houses, which they had marked for themselves in the daytime: they know not the light. For the morning is to them even as the shadow of death: if one know them, they are in the terrors of the shadow of death" (Job 24:12–17).

Bildad's reply in chapter 25 prompted this simple comment

from Job: "To whom hast thou uttered words?" (26:4).

People in the city do groan. They live in constant danger. Who will "utter words" to them? Who will take the gospel to the "inner city"? The Lord told his disciples that "a city that is set on a hill cannot be hid" (Matt. 5:14). The challenge is before us.

David and Marilyn Dolin are among the few who have not retreated from this difficult challenge. As their administrator, I have appreciated their dedication to a difficult assignment. It is a privilege to recommend this stirring missionary report. May the Lord use it to encourage a full home missions program in your local church!

Leigh E. Adams
Vice President
Baptist Mid-Missions

CHAPTER ONE

'Slave Owners'

When we think of slavery, especially slavery of the past, we associate it with the rural institution called the plantation. Slaves were dependent on plantation owners and were often controlled by fear. Although slavery was supposedly abolished by our government more than a hundred years ago, we find it flourishing today as it has never existed in the history of our country. The only difference in the slavery of the mid-1800s and that of today is ownership.

Today we have economic ownership instead, and perhaps many of the subjects are still controlled by fear. In yesteryear the slaves were primarily black, but today slavery is not characterized by one primary ethnic group. Any time slaves can be restricted in their mobility, they can be controlled. In the mid-1800s, the slave owners were usually landowners in certain geographic locations of our country. Today's counterparts are primarily located in the inner city.

Who are these unscrupulous "slave owners" that grip the inner city dwellers? They are many and they are merciless. Another question is, Can these slaves be freed? If so, how can this task be accomplished?

Although the great "slave owner" is commonly called "sin," he takes on many disguises such as unemployment. Our society places a great emphasis on success in the work world. When the family worker is unable to work steadily, the gratification derived by climbing the ladder of acceptability diminishes. Coupled with the man's alienation from God because of his spiritual condition, his unemployment soon causes his home to become a place of turmoil and unrest.

As we look at each one of these "slaves owners," we cannot help but see the underlying cause. The bond between the slave and his owner becomes as obvious as a metal chain and fetter—and just as effective. One of the greatest challenges is to convince slaves that they are slaves. Obviously a prisoner does not desire freedom until he first knows that he is incarcerated. Satan is not stupid. He knows that his slaves will clamor for freedom if they realize their peril. In order to remain a taskmaster, he disguises himself with many varied costumes. Religion, poverty, drugs, alcohol, immorality, venereal disease, mental disorder, witchcraft, gangs and murder are just a few of the costumes he wears.

The attitude of the inner city slave is to stay behind locked doors, but through the cracks in the walls we hear his cry for help. The more merciless the slave owner, the louder the cry.

Bound by a String of Beads

I first met Bob and Jan in their home. They were more fortunate than most because Bob was still employed. Bob and Jan had been raised in Roman Catholic homes and thus were raising their six-year-old son in their tradition. The family were not devout Catholics in the strictest sense of the word, but the three of them attended mass regularly.

Since Bob and Jan were heavily into drugs, their son was constantly exposed to their unsavory friends. This association raised within them enough concern to allow me to spend several evenings with them. Both were aware that their drug habits were unfulfilling and were destroying them. They constantly fought and would steal from one another to supply the money for their habits. Jan admitted that she had acceded to prostitution in order to support her habit and to help pay the rent on their house. My wife and I spent much time just talking with them before they began to see their real problem.

As we talked during the next several days, they agreed that their drug habits left them unsatisfied and full of guilt. As I directed the conversation toward Christ, they felt that I was talking about just another religion—and they believed they had enough religion to meet that need in their lives. We talked about prayer, and they agreed that it was necessary—but only to alleviate guilt. They did their praying by stroking beads and saying a certain number of "Hail Marys." The only common ground that was comfortable for each of us was our agreement that the Bible is the Word of God. Those who have never been bound by a string of beads cannot realize just how difficult it is to escape from this form of incarceration by Satan.

After I had visited their home several times, Bob and Jan both came under the convicting power of the Holy Spirit and trusted Christ as their Savior. They came to realize that there was more to Christianity than religion, and that salvation is in the Person of Jesus Christ and not in the church. Upon their confession of faith in Christ, their baptism by immersion and their coming into the fellowship of the church, we launched a ministry of freeing other inner-city slaves in Cleveland.

CHAPTER THREE

Death Was to Come at Midnight

The inner city is unique. No other place can match it for grandeur or passion. It can be a place of security, or it can be a concentration camp. When enclosed behind boundaries that are truly a home, one has a sense of peace. But out on the streets, and very often in some houses, there is turmoil and danger. Suburbia is a dream and really does not exist in the thinking of the inner-city dweller. Looming before him are invisible walls as effective as the Berlin Wall in preventing his escape.

There are two types of bricks that go into the building of these walls. One is conditioned thinking. The inner-city dweller reacts a certain way because it is all he knows. He must get up at a certain time, eat breakfast, dress a certain way, go to the bus stop, ride to the workplace, punch in, do assembly-line work over and over, eat lunch, go back and put the same parts in the same places, punch out, walk to the bus stop, get off at home, eat dinner, watch TV, go to bed and start the same routine again the next day. He does not think for himself because someone else does all the thinking for him. He becomes a human robot without a will or the ability to think, plan or innovate for himself.

The other type of brick in the invisible wall is fear. Unless a person has lived in a world that is controlled by fear, he cannot truly understand how effectively this fetter can paralyze and imprison an individual. Fear is of both the known and the unknown. The origin matters little; it is the results that are devastating to the individual.

If one is going to be delivered from the bondage of fear, he must realize who his enemy is, and he must also seek release from the captor. If he is not made aware that the enemy desires to hold him captive and that there is a way to escape his bondage, he will forever be a slave to his enemy. Satan is the master of deception. Sometimes he disguises himself, and at other times he openly reveals that he is the subjugator. He is a mighty foe, but he is not deity.

One of the major problems a slave of Satan has is that he is not even aware he has been immured by the enemy. The first step in releasing the inner-city inmate is to isolate him from other slaves. Once he is made aware of his captivity, he will entertain thoughts of escape. However, escape does not always free him from the scars his owner inflicted upon him.

The slave owner often wears many cloaks. Sometimes the raiment is so camouflaged that it is difficult even to detect the enemy. He can even be a professing Christian. As long as someone seems to be afloat in his Christianity, we seem to swim on the surface and leave alone that which is in the bathyal zone (subsurface).

We Christians are quick to quote 2 Corinthians 5:17: "Therefore if any man be in Christ, he is a new creature: old things are passed away; behold, all things are become new." While this is true, we must remember that when Lazarus was raised from the dead by Jesus Christ, he still had the old grave clothes on, and Jesus instructed His disciples to remove them. In the spiritual realm, grave clothes can sometimes be removed quickly and efficiently, but at other times they are difficult to remove when the new creature refuses to acknowledge their existence.

Several years ago a family came to the United States from Puerto Rico and settled in Cleveland. There were twenty-five brothers and sisters, but the mother and father had never bothered to marry. I often witnessed to the family and soon became friends with them. It seems there was always something they needed to borrow—a rake, a shovel, a hose or some tools. It was difficult to communicate with some of them because of the language barrier, while others of the family had a fine command of the English language.

Although we were friends, they would never come to church— their priest had forbidden it. The problem we faced was how to segregate these people from their subjugator. In this case, I believe that the process was set in motion by neighborly friendship without the demands often put upon Satan's slaves.

I have been admonished by teachers, preachers and peers that the emancipator must rush into a relationship with a slave with the attitude that "either you accept this proposal, or I'll go somewhere else and offer another person deliverance."

The approach is something of this nature: The person is either saved or lost. Since he is obviously lost, here is his rescue. The Romans' Road of the Bible will be pointed to hurriedly, with the attitude, Do you accept this or reject it? This example may be somewhat satirical, but it happens. Those who actually advocate such an attitude often do more to strengthen the enemy's grip than to loosen his hold.

One Sunday night, a little before midnight, two of the sisters began frantically pounding on my door. When I answered it, I could see they were in tears and visibly agitated. They told me that their brother was going to die at twelve o'clock. I asked them how they knew the hour, and they said that the devil had said so. They asked me to come quickly, as there was not time to secure a priest. They added that he probably would not come at such a late hour anyway, especially not out on the streets of the near-west side. I assured them I would be right there. I felt a strange moving of the Holy Spirit as I picked up my Bible and started walking down the street. As I stepped upon their porch, I looked at my watch. It was one minute to midnight.

I had prayed constantly since the two sisters had left and felt led by the Lord to wait until midnight before knocking on the door. At precisely midnight, I knocked and was immediately ushered into the house. As I was taken to the bedroom, I noticed three bizarre-looking men in the kitchen. They were wearing robes much like the Catholic priests wear. Their robes were white; their collars were red; and they wore black skullcaps. They also wore crimson sashes around their waists. "Who are they?" I whispered after we had passed them. "Warlocks," came the hushed reply.

As I entered the bedroom, the first thing I saw was the mother of Julio (not his real name), kneeling at the bedside, stroking a string of beads and praying, "Hail Mary, full of grace, please don't let my son die!" She had already said more than a thousand "Hail Marys," I was to learn later. I asked her to please leave the room.

I turned to Julio and noticed that he had taken off all of his clothes and was lying on the bed with his hands folded across his midsection. His eyes were closed, and he was sweating profusely even though the room was very cold. I began to talk to him, and the following is as close to the conversation as I can recall it.

"Julio, what is the matter?"/"I am going to die at midnight."/ "Who told you that you were going to die?"/"Satan."/"Do you want to know Satan's other name?"/"Yes."/"He is known as the Father of Lies. Do you know why God called him that?"/"Why?"/ "Look at your watch." It was two minutes past midnight. Julio was really shocked.

"Julio, Satan is after you. Do you know that?"/"Yes."/"Do you know what he wants with you?"/"To kill me."/"Yes, but what else?"/"I don't know."/"He wants you to burn in Hell forever. Do you want to escape from Satan?"/"Yes."/I placed a sheet over him and asked him to sit up. He was shaking uncontrollably.

"Julio, Jesus Christ can free you from Satan. He came into this world to defeat Satan and to provide you a way to escape from him and Hell, the Lake of Fire. Every person is born under Satan's control, but there is a way to escape for anyone who wants to do so. Physical death is nothing more than a doorway through which we enter into eternity. Once you pass through that door, there is no returning; you are in eternity forever. But God loves you and does not want you to enter into eternal damnation. He sent His only and sinless Son Jesus Christ to take your punishment through His death on the cross, His burial and His resurrection. This salvation is God's gift to you."

"How much does His salvation cost?" Julio asked. "I don't have very much money." (He asked this question because the Catholic church usually requires some monetary compensation for services rendered.)/"It doesn't cost you anything," I answered, "but it cost God everything. Would you like to escape from Satan?"/"Yes."/ "Look with me a moment at some verses in the Bible. Do you believe this is God's Word?"/"Yes."/"Why?"/"I have been told that."/"Would you rather believe God's Word or Satan's word that you heard tonight?"/"God's Word."/"Why?"/"Because Satan has already lied to me tonight."

"OK, Julio, I want you to stop me if I show you something that you don't understand. This could be the most important hour of your life. Now, let us look first at John 3:36: 'He that believeth on the Son hath everlasting life: and he that believeth not the Son shall not see life; but the wrath of God abideth on him.' Do you understand what God is saying?"/"Yes, if I don't believe in His Son, I will never have eternal life."/"That's right, Julio. Jesus wants to save you, but if He is going to save you, you must realize that you need to be saved. By that I mean that you need to know that you must be rescued from Satan; otherwise, you will never trust Jesus to save you. Why do you need to be saved?"/"Because the devil is going to get me."/"How do you know this?"/"He told me so."/"When?"/ "Tonight, in a seance."/"What did he say?"/"He said that I would die at midnight and I would forever be with him. I am going to Hell and I cannot do anything about it."/"Julio, that's exactly what you must realize if you are ever going to be saved. You cannot do anything about it, but there is One Who can. Would you like to know what God did for those who are in the same situation as you are?"/"Yes."

"Notice with me what God says in Romans 10:9–13: 'That if thou shalt confess with thy mouth the Lord Jesus, and shalt believe in thine heart that God hath raised him from the dead, thou shalt be saved. For with the heart man believeth unto righteousness; and with the mouth confession is made unto salvation. For the scripture saith, Whosoever believeth on him shall not be ashamed. For there is no difference between the Jew and the Greek: for the same Lord over all is rich unto all that call upon him. For whosoever shall call upon the name of the Lord shall be saved.'

"If we are willing to believe that Jesus died in our place, that He was buried and that He rose from the dead, He will save us. You see, Julio, Jesus overcame physical death. That death is the door to eternity. Now the Bible talks of another death, and that is spiritual death. Spiritual death is separation from God. Jesus overcame this death also. From the minute he is born, a person, even though he is physically alive, is spiritually dead. This is the result of sin. We have all sinned against God. The Bible tells us so right here in Romans 3:23: 'For all have sinned, and come short of the glory of God.' It also tells us the results of this sin in Romans 6:23: 'For the wages of sin is death; but the gift of God is eternal life through Jesus Christ our Lord.'

"This verse is talking about spiritual death. By spiritual death,

God means being dead in our spirits. If we are dead, then the only way that we can have life is to be made alive again. In order to be made alive again, we must be born again. Have you ever heard the expression 'being born again'?"/"Yes."/"Do you know what it means to be born again?"/"No."/"It means that we are given new life by Jesus Christ, or made alive in our spirit. When we realize that we are dead in sin and that Jesus Christ died on the cross to pay for our sin, and we call on Him to save us from our sin, then He will. We are dead spiritually, and He gives us life in Him. We are reborn by believing in Him. Nothing else. You see, Julio, we do not call upon Him unless we believe that He can and will save us. If we believe this, it is faith. It is through this faith that we are saved.

"Notice the last part of the verse we just read, 'the gift of God is eternal life through Jesus Christ our Lord.' Do you understand what a gift is?"/"Yes."/"What?"/"That means when someone gives you something with no strings attached."/"Right. Now, in order to have this gift of salvation, you must realize you need it and be willing to receive it. Let's again notice Romans 10:13: 'For whosoever shall call upon the name of the Lord shall be saved.' Do you need to be saved?"/"Yes."/"Do you want to be saved?"/"Yes."/"Why?"/"I have sinned like the Bible says, and the Devil is going to get me!"/ "Do you believe the Bible when it says that God will save you if you ask Him to?"/"Yes."/"Will He save you right now?"/"Yes."/ "How do you know this?"/"He said He would right there." Julio pointed to Romans 10:13.

"Julio, let's get down on our knees and ask Him to save you." The man got down on his knees and poured out his heart to God. He confessed that he was a sinner and "a gonner for sure," and he said, "Lord, the best that I know how, I'm asking you to come into my heart and save me."

At that very moment we heard a loud commotion coming from the kitchen; the door was slammed with such force that it shook the whole house. Upon investigating, we learned that the three war-locks had stormed out of the house, screaming profanities as they went. They could not have heard our conversation, but somehow they knew that Satan had lost another soul.

Even though we rejoiced in Julio's salvation, we found that the grave clothes do not always come off easily. The new creature was still shrouded in the cloak of Catholicism, perhaps harder to re-move than the yards and yards of linen that encased Lazarus' body. As long as the grave clothes remain, the mobility of the new Christian is limited, and his growth is restricted.

Julio's mind is confined to an intellectual straitjacket. Romanism has molded his mind to reject any teachings that salvation can be found outside the Roman Catholic church. This doctrine had been nourished in Julio from early childhood, until by the time he was twenty-five, it had been deeply ingrained. Julio finds it much easier to believe that his confusion is a result of his lack of faith in the Roman church rather than that the church is teaching erroneous doctrine.

The slave owner, dressed in a Roman Catholic uniform, has a firm grip on his prey. We have found that his grip can be loosened, but it takes much patience and praying. The crowbar is the Word of God. The indwelling Holy Spirit keeps reminding Julio that the Word of God is absolute truth, and that the teachings of the Roman church are not infallible. Slowly, ever so slowly, the grave clothes are coming off. Oh, how we are reminded of our Savior's words, "Loose him, and let him go."

CHAPTER FOUR

God Still Has 'She Bears'

O ur thinking is sometimes channeled as though it were the bed of a running stream. It is often hard to escape the high banks that border our thought patterns.

When we think of fear, we often associate it with some known factor that looms before us from the dark recesses of the unknown. Rarely do we stop to analyze its source so that we can effectively combat it. Perhaps fear is more noticeable in the city because of the greater concentration of people.

Within our city boundaries lies a world that suburbia seldom dreams of. It is a world within a world—so far removed that few people know of its existence. Often those who live there are not aware of it, for they keep themselves locked away behind barred doors. Closed doors and locked doors differ in every respect. Closed doors can be opened without a great deal of effort, but locked doors must be unlocked or broken down. Those who live behind locked doors live in fear. Fear is a vicious slave owner. If we are going to penetrate locked doors, we must be guided by the Holy Spirit; and we must use the Word of God wisely, or the person behind the door will never be freed from his prison house.

Few understand unemployment as the inner-city dweller does. Unemployment is miserable—so miserable, in fact, that it breeds contempt for those who are gainfully employed. Within the people develops an attitude that dictates their lives to the point of destroying everything that they once stood for.

Death becomes a way of life—not just to the body, but to anything. Anything that can be destroyed should be destroyed, whether it is of flesh or of material substance. Some people call it vandalism. The law of the concrete jungle is, "If you can't tear it down, deface it with graffiti; if it has a lock on it, break it open and steal the contents."

Unemployment often causes the mind to become programmed to a very low voice that says: "The world owes me something, and I'm going to get it." Those falling for this reasoning do not have any sympathy for those whom they are hurting. It is little wonder that there is so much crime in the inner city. The major reason for it is idleness. Someone aptly stated, "An idle mind is the Devil's workshop." If there isn't anything to do, then one will create his own form of recreation—and it is usually of a violent nature.

Psychologists try to separate the natures of individuals and place them into different categories. I believe that vandalism is just violence waiting to erupt. One group puts their mark or logo upon a structure, and another dislikes it and covers it with their own. Now you have the makings for a violent gang war. This reaction is brought on by idleness, and the idleness is a product of unemployment, and unemployment is the disclosed disguise of sin, which is controlled by the brutal taskmaster, Satan.

Employment causes one to keep a regular schedule and forces one person to answer to another. After someone has been unemployed for a period of time, he begins to develop a certain lifestyle. From this development arises an attitude. This proclivity dictates to that person that he does not have to answer to anyone, especially to someone with civil authority.

Now the law becomes a challenge. Instead of striving to live within the law, the attitude directs the person to live outside the law. Welfare, a part of the government, is something he takes because it is there to be had, not because he respects it. He can live "comfortably" because the state is a big brother who does not know how to deal with him. The state figures that if it carries him along for a while, he will become a good citizen and will soon get a job.

In Cleveland, one city father claims that gangs do not exist in his city. Perhaps this claim is made in order to reassure citizens who might venture into the city to shop. For whatever reason this claim is made, it is only wishful thinking. The truth is that there are many gangs scattered throughout every major city.

A local television station did a special report on gang activity in Cleveland, and it reported that there are from fifty to seventy-five gangs active throughout the city. Most of the gangs are small, but our own area alone has at least three large ones.

Also, in any large city, ethnic citizens tend to stick together in various neighborhoods. This is not to say that all the people of the same neighborhood belong to a certain ethnic group, but nevertheless one finds more of one nationality in certain sections than in others. In our neighborhood, there is a large concentration of people from Puerto Rico and from the hills of West Virginia, Pennsylvania, Tennessee and Kentucky. Why these particular groups have settled together, I have never been able to determine.

The streets that a certain gang claims are called "turfs," and usually everyone in the area knows who owns them. A member of one gang does not venture onto the turf of an opposing gang. The turfs are marked by graffiti, and if one gang writes over that graffiti, that action alone is enough to trigger war. Usually war occurs only between two rival gangs and rarely involves others; therefore, few outside the gang know about the rumble (fight). One of the problems with gangs is that anyone may become their entertainment for the day. Each member of the gang is eager to demonstrate to the others how tough he is. Two or three gang members may beat up an innocent person just because he was in their path. Gangs stage robberies and purse-snatchings. The money is usually used to buy drugs and alcohol. The gang members pay for their drugs because they can "rip off" a dealer only one time. Before the day ends, the rip-off person is usually dead. More often than not, drug dealers are protected by big-time hoods who frown on small-time hoods trying to rip off "their people."

The problems found on the streets of a large city may not necessarily come from gangs. Plenty of individuals are out there just waiting to do anything that strikes their fancy. One can find himself in a perilous situation at almost any moment while on the street.

Just before we left Mobile, Alabama, to come to Cleveland, someone gave us a Doberman Pinscher. We decided that in order to best utilize God's provision of the dog, we should at least get him into obedience training so that we could control him when people were around him. Klipper responded well to his training. He is very aggressive upon command and very gentle when told, "Klipper, everything is okay." Someone may suggest that in using a dog we are not trusting God for His protection. But we should remember how God used the two she bears to protect Elisha when he was being harassed (2 Kings 2:23, 24). God protects those whom He calls to a particular ministry. He also issues those individuals another asset; it is called "common sense." My family and I have had several encounters with gangs and with dangerous individuals, but thanks to God's provision of Klipper, we have never been physically harmed.

Most people do not spend as much time on the streets as I do. I do not recall a single night since I have been in the city that I have not been on the streets. The only way to really know one's neighborhood is to spend time walking in it. So each night, regardless of the weather, I walk Klipper and visit people on the street. Our neighborhood is noted as one of the highest crime rate areas in the city. At any time of the day or night, something is going on. Burglaries, muggings, murder, robbery, rape and battery are not limited to the cover of darkness.

One morning, about four o'clock, Klipper became extremely agitated and with a snarl tore downstairs. The burglars who were trying to break in were able to close the window that they had pried open and thus escaped Klipper's wrath. We heard the window slam, and when we rushed downstairs, we were just in time to see two men running across the street and down the alley. It was fortunate for them that they had not broken the window, or Klipper would probably have hurled himself after them. The same thing happened during the daytime, only this time it was the back door they pried open. They never did get the door closed, but they did manage to keep the storm door between themselves and Klipper.

I mentioned these two incidents at the school where Klipper was being trained. At about the same time, a major television network was doing a special news story about dogs used for protection. When the obedience school reported the success of one of the dogs they were training (Klipper), the network contacted us and arranged for an interview. It turned out to be a forty-five minute session that was aired nationally. I was able to tell why my family was in this area of the city. The network edited out none of the things we said about our work. Some of the questions the reporters asked were, "Why are you in this area?" "How do you know that

God has directed you here?" and "Where were you before you came here, and what was your work there?" During the interview, I demonstrated how Klipper obeyed commands, and I simulated attacks. The reporters even had a cameraman try to get through the window that the thieves had tried to enter, and Klipper again showed how he had protected our home. Via this means, the entire nation was made aware that someone was at work among the inner-city people. One of the questions the interviewers asked was, "How can a man be changed on the inside?" This question was prompted by my remark that a man cannot be changed by incarceration—that if he is ever going to be changed, he must be changed on the inside. They did not edit out my reply as I told them how a person is born again.

The obedience school wanted to use parts of the film for advertising. However, they did not want to become involved with royalties, so they offered us a contract to give Klipper what they termed "super dog" training in exchange for the rights to the film. We consented, and they gave the dog fifteen hundred dollars of additional training at no cost to us. He is perhaps one of the best-trained dogs in Cleveland.

We know of at least two more times that burglars have attempted to enter our home. On each occasion, Klipper has convinced them that there was easier prey in the neighborhood. While he has never bitten anyone, few are convinced that he would not do so if he thought it necessary.

He becomes extremely vicious upon command and completely docile when I or a member of my family tells him that everything is okay. I would be apprehensive about leaving my family alone at night if he were not on the premises. Everyone in the neighborhood knows him, so it is doubtful that the burglars who visited us were from our neighborhood. We also have a female Doberman, Lady, that we took in off the streets, and she copies everything that Klipper does. This works out well because when I am on the street with Klipper, Lady is home watching over my family.

One evening while Klipper and I were walking down the street, we were confronted by one of the gangs in the area. They decided that I was going to be the object of their entertainment. I had seen them coming and started to go back the way I had come. Another group was coming up behind me. Their leader informed me of their intentions. I told him that it was not in their best interest to cause me physical harm. He insisted, "I'm going to whip you *and* your dog." I knew that the only recourse I had was to convince him otherwise. I took a good grip on Klipper's leash and gave him the attack command. He began lunging at them and became so excited that he was actually throwing slobber upon them. It did not take Klipper long to convince them to look elsewhere for a victim. There is something about a lunging, snarling Doberman that causes even the most malevolent person to quail and cringe.

Another evening as I was walking Klipper, I could not help but notice the odd shape of a man coming down the street. He was hunched over and sort of shuffled or lumbered, more like an animal than a man. In his hands was a piece of pipe about four feet long. As he drew closer, he began to slow down, then stopped in front of us and began to threaten me with the pipe. Although he never said a word, he was hissing and feigning swings with the pipe. Spittle ran down his chin. The look in his eyes was that of a rabid animal. It was very cold that evening, with the temperature and wind chill factor about thirty degrees below zero. But he was wearing a very light jacket, and the cold did not seem to affect him.

I pleaded with him to let me pass, turn around or go around him. He did not reply but just kept threatening and hissing. The froth on his face was frozen, and the front of his jacket was covered with frozen spittle. For the first time since I had come to Cleveland, I knew real fear in my heart. This was not an ordinary encounter; this was a crazed person I was facing, and I could not communicate with him or get any sort of response from him, nor could I even distinguish whether or not he had heard me.

Besides praying, I did the only other thing I knew. I gave Klipper his attack command. The dog immediately began to lunge at the man. I did not release the leash but kept a tight grip on it. The vicious attack must have penetrated the man's mind because he turned his attention toward the dog and away from me. Although I kept Klipper on attack, I began to drag him into the street and around the man. He kept threatening the dog with the pipe, but he never did swing it. After we had got around him, we were able to continue down the street. The man turned into some bushes and disappeared from our view. I have been in some tough situations, but that is the most fear I have ever known.

Those who live in, and are controlled by, fear sometimes react spontaneously to situations without thought as to their actions. The only law that controls them is a fear greater than the governor of their lives. Although we are confident of God's presence with us while working in the inner city and reassured by the constant presence of Klipper, we are still in a precarious situation. The large gangs have little regard for a minister, and the presence of a dog is not much of a deterrent. Since most gangs are armed with pistols, knives, clubs and chains, they can overpower a dog. Klipper is protection against four or five men. When you are facing ten to twenty gang members, you must have something else to defend with. There are anywhere from seventy-five to about two hundred gang members in the "Latin Knights," and the "Sir Mingo Dogs" and the "Saviours" are about the same size. But God gave me another "she bear."

One afternoon as I was driving down the street, one of the roughest characters I have ever laid eyes on came out of a restaurant parking lot on his motorcycle. As he made a turn onto the street, the wheels of his cycle slipped out from under him, and he went down. My first reaction was to act as though I had not noticed him and go on my way. However, at the same moment, these thoughts crossed my mind, and the Holy Spirit spoke to me: "If you pass this man by, he will never hear a clear presentation of the gospel, will die and will go into an eternal Hell." I stopped, went over to him and held his bike up while he worked on it to get it going again. He could not understand why I was helping him, especially since he was wearing his "colors." He stood back and asked me, "What's your bag, man?" I told him that my bag was Jesus Christ and His provision of eternal life for him. "Do you know that one day He died in your place?"/"Why?"/"Because He loves you."/"Ain't nobody that loves me that much."

I invited him to come to the little church on the corner. He said, "What would your people do if we all showed up on Sunday morning?" I told him that they would probably run for their lives, but that I would sit them down and preach to him and his friends just as I would to anyone else who came to the church.

The next day I heard the roar of engines vibrating my whole house. I looked out my window and saw between forty and fifty Hell's Angels by my fence. The whole neighborhood was vibrating by this time as they raced their engines. They were drinking beer and smoking dope and doing wheelies. Suddenly the streets were deserted of everyone but the gang.

I thought my end had come; I prayed and asked God to protect my family. These men were more animal than human and had total disregard for everyone and everything but their own lust. After claiming the promise of Joshua 1:9, I went out to the fence to keep them from harming my family. I found that the "Angel" I had befriended, Stan, just wanted to chat for a minute. No one but Stan said a word to me. The others seemed to be interested in their own world.

They began to drop by two or three times a week. Sometimes there would be three and sometimes as many as fifty. The whole neighborhood was aware they were coming to my house on a regular basis because of the tremendous disturbance they caused. Little did I realize that God had directed them my way. Often we think of the Hell's Angels as being bent on destruction at all times. But the only thing that they did was throw beer cans all over. I am reminded of some words that Joseph spoke about his brothers, "Ye thought evil against me; but God meant it unto good" (Gen. 50:20).

I marvel at the hand of God and His protective custody. The street gangs suddenly seemed to look upon me in a different light. They did not know what my connection with the Hell's Angels was, and they were not about to give me trouble for fear of retribution from the Angels. The rumor is, if you cross the Angels or infringe upon their territory, you are dead. There is never a settlement, never any negotiations, never a fight. Right or wrong, it is the twelve-gauge shotgun that does the talking. Perhaps gangs form because of fear and self-preservation, but they are controlled by the greater fear of annihilation.

After a period of about three months, Stan finally agreed to meet me at a restaurant for coffee. During our second visit, I had the privilege of leading him to Christ. We then went to his house and led his wife to Christ. Stan was one of the few Angels who was actually married, and he and his wife had two precious little girls.

A member does not simply resign from the Angels or quit running with them. If he does, he will meet with an untimely end. In order for Stan to disassociate himself with his former gang, he had to deceive them. He let it be known that he was going to Phoenix, Arizona. He left Cleveland, dumped his cycle somewhere and then came back to Cleveland. The Angels in Phoenix had never heard of Stan, and the ones in Cleveland were not looking for him. He moved to our neighborhood and began to live for the Lord.

After more than one year of faithful service, it was evident from his testimony that he loved his Savior. One afternoon as Stan was walking down the street, a young man ran a stop sign on his motorcycle and hit a car broadside. The cycle careened wildly upon the sidewalk. The handlebar of the bike hit and entered Stan in his lower back. The same day, he was ushered into the presence of the Savior he had grown to love. I could not help but reflect upon these words, "He that lives by the sword shall also die by the sword." Today there is an "Angel" in Heaven.

CHAPTER FIVE

Manumission— Almost?

One evening, Jean (not her real name) came to me with a story that tore my heart out. She needed bus fare to go to West Virginia to try to find and bring back her sixteen-year-old daughter who had run away with a man who had abandoned her on the streets of a large city in that state. Jean felt that if she could find the girl, she could convince her to return home. Jean offered to reimburse the church for the bus ticket just as soon as her welfare check came. I knew some of the difficulty a young girl could encounter if she were left to fend for herself on the streets, so I gave her the money out of my own pocket.

The next evening I received a collect call from Jean, and she told me that she had found her daughter. However, the relatives she had hoped to borrow money from had moved, and she did not know to where. She needed bus fare for herself and her daughter to get back to Cleveland. She said that they had tried to borrow money for bus fare from the churches in that city, but each one had turned them down. Now I was really involved and felt that I could not abandon them in a city where they knew no one and had no shelter. I went down to the bus station and prepaid a ticket for their return. (Later I explained to Jean that most churches have been taken by shysters so many times that they sometimes become callous. It is difficult sometimes to determine who is legitimate and who is not.)

After I had prepaid their tickets, I called them back to let them know they could pick up the tickets. I met them at the bus station in Cleveland the next day. We immediately began counseling sessions, and the girl told me she liked older men and planned to find another one just as soon as she could. She did—and took off for Texas two days later. Her mother was distraught over the whole situation. Since I was now involved with the family, I had an opportunity to talk with all of the other family members.

Jean's twelve-year-old son was an admitted homosexual. The boy was having an affair with a thirty-seven-year-old man and said that he liked the man—maybe even "loved" him. Also, he had every intention of continuing the relationship. He told his mother that he would kill her if she reported the affair to the authorities. I tried to talk to David and show him from the Bible that this was not a matter of preference—it was sin. He claimed to be an atheist, and it was easy to detect that he had been thoroughly indoctrinated by the man with whom he was living. As we continued to talk, I realized I was involved with a family bound by perversion.

Jean's other children began to tell me about themselves. The fourteen-year-old daughter was a lesbian and did not care who knew it. The eighteen-year-old brother was a drug addict and well on his way to a life of crime to support his habit. These children had been brought up in a Pentecostal home, and to them religion was a farce. They had seen it all their young lives. There were several weeks at a time when the mother would read her Bible constantly and "pray in unknown tongues." Soon this religious kick, they said, would degenerate into bouts of cursing and drunkenness. She would leave her children alone for hours while she was in the other room with some man. The twelve-year-old claimed that his first experience with homosexuality was with the Pentecostal preacher. Whether or not this was true, I was never able to substantiate, but I have no reason to disbelieve him as he seemed to be telling the truth about everything else and had no reason to lie. He was not trying to justify his preference; he was proud of his lifestyle.

Jean was acting like a mother distraught over her children's sins, and she claimed to love the Lord. She assured me that she was a born-again Christian. When I eventually told her that I did not have any more money to give her but that I would try to get some food to last until the end of the month, she began to curse me. Profanity rolled from her mouth like water down a waterfall. The more I talked to her, the more I became convinced that she was probably demon possessed. She, too, was a slave bound by the cords of sin with which Satan had tied her.

Some time passed before I was again involved with the family. The mother called me on the phone, and I refused to come over, but I told her that I would spend some time on the telephone with her. I recorded the conversation as accurately as I could and will share it with you.

"Preacher, what am I going to do? We just returned from the doctor, and David has AIDS." As we talked, she began to describe the symptoms that he had. "He has a constant fever and is on the verge of pneumonia. He has lost twenty-five pounds in the last six weeks and has constant diarrhea. He can't seem to remember things for more than a few minutes and has these little tumors all over his stomach and legs. He had been living with this man for a long time, but eight weeks ago the man left, and David doesn't know where he is. Since then he has been with just any man who will have sex with him. It seems that he is obsessed with sex. If he is in the house, he is always looking at dirty books with pictures in them of men doing all sorts of things. At other times he wants to be with some man. In the last two weeks he has gotten really bad. He can hardly get out of bed or off of the couch. These men come to see him and bring him marijuana, which he says he needs.

He is always saying that he is going to kill me and himself. When he is able to get up, he steals things out of the house or brings something home that he has stolen somewhere else. He lies to me all the time and curses God for his problems. He took a knife and stabbed my Bible many times—and then he burned it. Brother Dolin, I really need for you to come and talk with him."

I told her that I would talk to him by phone but that I could not come to the house. As we talked, I learned from her that one of her daughters, who was seventeen, had had three abortions and had been arrested for prostitution on several occasions. Her nineteen-year-old son was in a penitentiary. Her fifteen-year-old daughter was involved with a lesbian and was heavily into drugs.

Jean said that she wanted to get back into church but needed some clothes to wear. She also said she needed some money to get her gas and electricity turned back on and to buy some food because they didn't have anything. She had a sister in West Virginia and a brother who was in jail.

My heart breaks for this family, but I cannot help them. When you read these lines, David will be with his slavemaster, Satan. I talked briefly by phone with him, and he informed me that he "hated" God.

There are times when one feels so helpless and frustrated; perhaps this is the compelling force that drives me on.

This is not an isolated case. The only difference in it and others are the surrounding circumstances and the people involved. Satan has the inner-city dwellers so bound with the cords of sin that escape is virtually impossible. Today, tomorrow or the next day I know that I will again enter into the life of a family who are the slaves of Satan, and I become encouraged because perhaps this time they will allow Jesus Christ to sever the bonds that trammel their souls.

CHAPTER SIX

Supermarket of Drugs

Suburbanites sometimes hear and read about kids in the local high school being involved with drugs and how some of them are arrested during a raid. This is as close as most of us get to the drug problem. It is not often that you find drugs being dealt with like a supermarket selling groceries. It is hard to believe that you could see as many as twenty cars stopped, blocking traffic and buying drugs. This is not an uncommon sight in our cities. Drugs are sold openly and almost without restraint. When we first came to Cleveland, I was astonished that the drug dealers could operate so openly without fear of arrest.

This openness of drug dealing is not restricted to one area of the city, and it goes on twenty-four hours a day. In our neighborhood, there were dealers using our church steps to sit on while dealing, and there was not a time, day or night, when some type of deal was not going on. I knew that if I threatened them, I would suffer the consequences. Also, if you desire to win them to the Lord, you cannot have the reputation of being a "fink." What do you do? Do you ignore the dealing, run them off or call the police? I decided that none of those approaches was the answer. The best approach was to preach to them. As they congregated on the church property, I appeared with my Bible and held a preaching service.

Of course Klipper, who is my constant companion on the streets, would be right there with me as I proclaimed the gospel to them. I suppose that Klipper has heard more gospel preaching than any dog alive. My mingling with the Bible open among these drug dealers and buyers had an unsettling effect upon them. Suddenly they would remember that they had something else to do. Even the ones who did not have a mother would suddenly have to go to the store for her. Any excuse was used to get away from the sound of the gospel. This gang of drug dealers finally decided that there must be a better place to deal drugs than on our corner. They moved down the street a block to avoid my constant preaching.

The corner of West Fifty-second Street and Bridge Avenue was always a beehive of activity. Drugs and prostitution were on a rampage. Sometimes it would take fifteen minutes to work one's way through the traffic at this intersection. People would be lined up just like at the supermarket check-out line to buy drugs. It seemed that even when the police did make a few arrests and the police car was still in sight taking away those who had been arrested, more drug dealers would take their place. Then those who had been arrested would be back on the corner selling drugs again that same day. What a mockery this was.

Finally, the residents of that area became so enraged and put so much pressure on the politicians that the woman who was known as the Queen of West 52nd Street was arrested. She had been arrested so many times that it was said she knew the precinct police by their first names. When the Queen went before the judge this time, he noted that she had twenty-nine prior arrests for drug dealing and operating a prostitution ring. She was convicted and sentenced to three hundred and sixty to six hundred years in prison. She will be eligible for parole in thirty years. By then she will be seventy-four years old and probably out of commission. Drugs are still big business in our neighborhood, but not to the extent they once were. With the closure of this operation, our neighborhood improved considerably.

Even with curtailments being placed upon the use of one of the weapons from Satan's arsenal, we are still faced with the same problems because he is so persistent in his efforts to control the masses. I don't believe that we will ever see the majority of the people who live in the inner city rescued from his impoundment. But if we have persistency and patience, God can use us to release some.

Go, and Sin No More

believe that a Bible message should be well planned and structured to move smoothly during the preaching hour. I also believe that the Holy Spirit moves the service as He desires, and that we must be careful not to be so organized that we do not leave room for Him to work in our midst. I try to prepare myself with study and prayer before I enter the pulpit, and I believe that God leads me on the contents of the message well before the service begins. Thus I enter the pulpit with confidence that the message I preach will be the message that God wants me to deliver to the congregation. But I will never forget the night that God prompted me to change the message after I arrived at the church, and it has had a profound effect upon my confidence as to God's leading. After reading the text, I felt a strange moving of the Spirit of God upon my soul. Immediately we went to prayer, and I asked the congregation to please turn to the text, "The effectual fervent prayer of a righteous man availeth much." I apologized that I did not know the exact verse number but told them that it was in the book of James. From that moment on, the words seemed to flow, and I cannot even remember what I said. At the end of the service, a lady who was small in stature came forward in response to the invitation. She was a mess. Both of her eyes were black, and her lip had been cut all the way through by her tooth as a result of being hit with a fist. She was crying and asked that the church please pray for her husband, so we asked that the entire congregation gather around the altar to pray for him. The praying lasted almost an hour. Just before we closed the service, I told her that I would be by to visit her husband the next morning.

Around ten o'clock the next day, I knocked on her door. Her husband answered. As soon as I told him who I was, he slammed the door in my face and, with a curse, swung at that precious little lady at the same time. I stuck my foot in the door to catch it because I did not want her to take another beating on my account. I figured that if he beat up on anyone that morning, it might as well be me.

I said, "Sir, I came to talk to you, and I am not going to leave until I do, so you might as well let me in." He did, after some conversation. I told him why I was there. I told him that I loved his soul and that Jesus loved him so much that He was willing to die for him. He had the strangest look on his face. It was as if he had never heard anything like this before. He didn't know what to say, so he ordered me to sit in a straight-backed chair directly in front of him—but across the room. He sat on the couch—directly in the middle. It did look strange. He ordered his wife out of the house and then said, "State your business and then get out." As far as I can recall, this is the only time that I have been impressed by God to give someone my full testimony as to what I was before God saved me. Every time I hear someone stand in church and begin to tell of the ugly sin he was involved in before he was saved, I cringe inside. It is enough to say, "I was a lost sinner, bound by the cords of sin." I feel that if we indulge in the details of our sin, we are glorifying Satan. As Christians we should never give Satan an opportunity to glory. I am ashamed of the life that I lived before I was saved. When I am reminded of my past life, I try to incorporate the words of the apostle Paul when he said, "Forgetting what is behind and straining torward what is ahead, I press on" (Phil. 3:13, NIV). Since no one else was present but the two of us, I gave in and related my past life to him, believing that I was impressed by the Holy Spirit to do so.

As I told him in more detail my story and how Christ had come into my life and how He saved me, I could see him begin to tremble. Tears formed in his eyes and flowed down his cheeks. In just a few minutes, he fell across the coffee table and cried out for Christ to save him also. When he finished asking Jesus to save him, I noticed the handle of a thirty-eight caliber revolver sticking out from the cushion where he had been sitting.

After Jack was saved, he began to tell me his story. He had served thirty-eight years in the state penitentiary for the murder of three men. He said that he had been a gambler and had always won, for if he didn't have the cards to win, he would pull his gun and take the money anyway. If anyone protested, Jack would shoot him in the leg, and if there were further argument, Jack would probably kill him and the others so no one could say anything. He also confessed to the murder of another man for which he had never been tried and asked my advice as to what he must do.

I told him that after he was baptized Sunday evening, he must confess his crime to the authorities. Monday morning he went to see the state attorney general, as I told him not to go to the local police since he was under a federal parole at the time. The state's attorney general listened to his story about his conversion, his time in the state penitentiary and about the murder of the other man. The state's attorney general's words were: "I have seen what religion can do for a man, and I have seen our prison system fail. Religion is the most powerful force on earth. I have more cases with witnesses than I can get before a judge, and I don't have a witness to the murder you have confessed. My advice to you is to get out of here and live your religion." I couldn't help but be reminded of the words of our Savior when He said to the woman, "Go, and sin no more."

Jack did leave the official's office that morning, but he never did learn to live religion—he learned to *live Christ*. Jack today is a fervent soul-winner.He goes searching for the men who are "down-and-outers"; he looks for the losers; he mingles with the real "hard-core" and brings them to Christ. Jack feels that if Christ could forgive him, there is no one living who could not be saved if he were told of our Savior. My question is, Is there anything too hard for God?

CHAPTER EIGHT

Two Hundred Bullet Holes

Wouldn't it be nice if every story ended with a fair maiden marrying a handsome prince and living a happy life in utopia forever? In Christian service, we sometimes have happy endings; but sometimes Satan gleefully mocks us, and we seem to labor in vain.

One afternoon, as I sat in my study at the church, I was disturbed by some of the worst noise I have ever heard. I went to investigate and discovered that three "ghetto blasters" (radios) were blaring on three different rock stations. With these ghetto blasters were about ten girls ranging in age from around ten to sixteen. The language they were using would have made Satan himself blush.

As I observed them from a window just above their heads, I watched a man come out of the apartment building across the street and make his way toward the girls. One of them talked to him in low tones for a couple of minutes, then pulled some money from her jeans. I counted the money as she gave it to him—sixteen one-dollar bills. After he put the money in his pocket, he began to make her a "fix." I watched as he cooked the heroin in a bottle cap with a cigarette lighter and took a syringe out of his pocket and wiped it on his pant leg. He then filled it with the heroin from the bottle cap and gave it to the girl. I was not more than four feet from her as she injected it into her arm. I wish that I could give you a success story about winning her to the Lord, but the truth is that the fourteen-year-old died a couple of weeks later from a drug overdose. This is not an isolated case; it is a daily occurrence in the inner city.

In the time we have lived on West 52nd Street, there have been nine people killed in a certain apartment building not more than sixty feet from our house. Fights take place almost every day, bringing an ambulance and police cars to the scene.

One evening as I sat at my desk, I could hear gunshots outside and bullets hitting the walls of my office, but this is not unusual. I do not believe the people are shooting at us to scare us or to do personal harm. There are many bullet holes in the windows. Many times we have had to patch the roof because of bullet holes. In one two-week period, I patched more than two hundred bullet holes in the roof. We have since had bulletproof glass installed in the windows just in case someone should happen to be on the other side when the gunmen start shooting. Ninety percent of the shots are fired from the apartment building across the street. One's first reaction is that this must be too dangerous a place to live, but we are convinced that the center of God's will is the safest place on earth.

I do not share the last two paragraphs to draw sympathy or admiration. I want simply to give an idea of how desperately men are needed to take the gospel message to our large cities. Life is short in this environment—and very uncertain. Thousands of our big-city dwellers will never hear the gospel and be delivered from the incarceration that Satan has placed them in unless workers come to free them. Can you hear their pitiful cry as it seeps from the cracks in the sidewalks? Like stench from the sewer, their cry for help permeates the air.

CHAPTER NINE

Just Fourteen

The exhilaration we feel when one of Satan's slaves has been liberated can quickly change to exasperation. I am not one to become ebullient toward someone, but at times I have been so vehement inside that I have found it impossible without God's grace to control my temper. At times I have hated Satan so much that the passion of my soul was to murder him. I can understand why the laws of our land have recognized the motive—"a crime of passion."

We met Dee through another teen and began to work with her and her younger brother. Dee was a wild girl and was a street product. She confided to me one day after she was saved that she had sold herself to more than a hundred men for the money to buy drugs. Dee would steal anything she could get her hands on. At fourteen, she had already had many encounters with the police.

We could hear her cry for help as she desperately searched for love, attention and acceptance. We began to share with her how much Jesus Christ loved her and cared for her. Her interest was immediately kindled, and she always wanted to know more.

One Sunday morning she came down the aisle of our church with tears streaming down her cheeks. She said, "I want to have

Jesus in my heart and life." I have never witnessed such a radical change of a person so quickly. Dee fell in love with Jesus so much that He became her whole life. Her salvation resulted in several other teens getting saved as well as her ten-year-old brother.

One evening as we were in discipling class, I was trying to emphasize to these teens that the Bible is God's Word. That evening, Dee taught me one of the most precious truths I have ever known. As I held my Bible up before them I asked, "What is this?" Dee raised her hand, and I called on her expecting her to say, "That's the Bible" or "It's the Word of God." Instead she replied, "That's God speaking to us." As that truth sank into my heart, I could hardly contain myself.

Dee was a fervent witness for her newfound Savior and wanted everyone to love Him as she did. One Sunday Dee didn't come to church, and I went by her house to see her. I thought that she may have been sick. I was met by her mother who told me that Dee would never be coming to our church again. She said that she would rather have Dee the way she had formerly been than "to be full of religion. She's always preachin' Jesus to me, and I'm tired of it." Dee's mother had been brought up in church, but had long since become an alcoholic.

The combination of conviction over her sinfulness and the enslavement by Satan resulted in a hatred for anything to do with Christianity. She was living with a man not her husband, and they soon moved from our area, taking Dee with them. She forbade me to ever talk to, or visit with, her son or daughter again. I have never gotten over her hatefulness, and I didn't leave her until I had vented my broken heart upon her decision. Please pray for her as God brings her to your mind. Somewhere out there in this world she is in battle with Satan.

CHAPTER TEN

Friday, the 13th

Satan is a genius when it comes to prevaricating to mankind. He would have us believe the still common idea that witchcraft is practiced only in countries where education is the exception, not the rule. If we are told that human sacrifices are sometimes offered up to Satan in Haiti, we have little difficulty accepting it, but if we are told that it happens in our neighborhoods, we become skeptical.

Authorities in Toledo, Ohio, tried to expose this practice in 1985, but they were buffeted on every hand. There was much evidence to substantiate the accusations, but Satan was able to conceal the bodies that were offered; so the conclusion was that the occult was not operating there. But the conclusion was wrong: Satan is worshiped in this country, and human sacrifices are offered. Some of the children who are missing have been offered as human sacrifices, according to reliable sources.

It is much easier for Satan worshipers to operate in the large cities; the activities associated with Satan worship can be concealed because of the masses of people. I have had opportunities to become involved with those who are in peril, such as victims of rape, assault and robbery. It is unbelievable what takes place behind buildings, in alleyways or behind closed doors. Fear is the restraint Satan uses to fetter those who would come to the rescue.

I have often heard well-meaning citizens boast that they would readily come to the aid of someone who was being brutally stabbed on the sidewalk. Perhaps you have read in your newspaper that twenty or more people witnessed a violent crime being committed against an elderly person and no one came to his aid. It is impossible to understand the fear that restrained them unless you have lived in the realm where "fear is king."

One Wednesday evening two young people, almost paralyzed with fear, ran into our church. The twelve-year-old girl was wearing only the shirt of the fifteen-year-old boy, who in turn was clad only in his shoes and pants. They were so terror-stricken that it took some time before we could determine what the crisis was. As their story began to unfold, we could feel the presence of evil.

The young lad had purposely placed his life in jeopardy for the young girl. Across the street from us was a witch coven, a meeting place for Satan worship and witchcraft. There were twelve witches in this coven, and the thirteenth was to be embodied on the following Friday (the 13th). Before Satan will accept the thirteenth witch on Friday the 13th, a virgin sacrifice must be offered to him.

The twelve-year-old girl had been stripped nude and tied to an altar. She was to have a wooden stake driven through her genitals, to have had her heart cut out and eaten by the thirteenth witch and her body burned. The fifteen-year-old boy, wanting to rescue her, had managed to cut her loose, and they ran to the church for sanctuary.

Both of these young people had relatives living in another state, and we rushed them there after they had revealed their story to us. They barely escaped, as they were being sought by the coven. This did not happen in some jungle far away, but in Cleveland, Ohio!

The people of the inner city are desperate for someone who will heed their cries for help. Literally thousands of people are milling through the streets; yet the individuals could just as well be isolated on some forlorn island in the middle of the ocean, hundreds of miles from the nearest human. They have been isolated by Satan, and sin is the cell that keeps them in solitary confinement. There is only one way they will ever escape—someone, perhaps you, will bring them the message of pardon.

CHAPTER ELEVEN

Someone Has Stolen My Bible

Often we are faced with situations in the inner city where the answer to the many situations that develop in the lives of its people is circumvented by the conditions at hand. We do not always know what to do, so we must rely upon the Holy Spirit to guide us. There are no pat answers, and there are no conclusive statistics to reveal the percentage of "professors" of Christ who actually go on to spiritual maturity. Often we find it takes many weeks or months before a new Christian begins to shed his "old grave clothes" and grow in the Lord.

While I was visiting people on the street one afternoon, I met Maynard. I suppose I first noticed him because of his physique. He weighted 260 pounds and stood 6' 6" tall. As I passed him, I could see the desperation of his soul in his eyes.

As we began to talk, I learned that he was a drifter without any direction in mind. He was very mixed up and confused about life and didn't know what he was going to do. As we talked, I found a ray of hope deep within his being. He said that he had left St. Louis, Missouri, and had headed east. His wife had left him, and he had since lost all sense of time. He said no one cared for him, not even his parents. When he was fourteen they abandoned him. They did so by sending him to school one day; when he came home at the end of the day, they had moved.

Often he was picked up by the police, and the courts would place him in foster homes. Maynard would run away because the people generally had taken him in just for the money the state paid them for foster care. Somehow Maynard ended up in Texas where he worked in the oil fields. He met and married a young girl with a similar background. By the time Maynard was twenty-one years old, he had quite a résumé: abandoned by parents; junior-high dropout; runaway; police record; drug abuser; alcoholic; oil worker; married; two children; separated; drifter.

While hitchhiking just north of Columbus, Ohio, Maynard was picked up by a Christian young man. As they traveled northward, the Christian asked Maynard if he knew where he was going. Thinking the man was referring to a geographical location, Maynard said no. Turning the conversation toward spiritual matters with this reply, the Christian soon led Maynard to Christ. He dropped Maynard off in Cleveland, and this is where we encountered one another.

Maynard didn't have any money, and the clothes he wore were his only possessions. I detected sincerity in him and decided that he was not trying to con me. We found Maynard a place to stay, located clothing and found employment in a fast-food restaurant.

Maynard developed a hunger to know his newfound Savior better. He was faithful in coming to every service. Each evening he came to my house to study his Bible. Whenever the temptations of alcohol or drugs became overpowering, he came running. It didn't matter to him if it were 2:00 A.M.; he knew he needed help in order to keep from slipping back into Satan's slave market. We would pray, read from God's Word and talk until he was sure of the Lord's victory, and then he would go back to his apartment. He is one of the hungriest Christians for God's Word I have ever known.

One evening Maynard came to my house with one of the saddest stories I have ever heard. He looked as though he had just lost his best friend. He was so broken that it took a while for him to stop crying long enough to tell me what had happened. He said, "Someone stole my Bible from under my pillow while I was at work." He could understand their taking his money and clothes— but not his Bible.

I had just bought a new Bible, and it was still in the box. As we talked, I opened my desk drawer, took out the Bible and handed it to him. His face lit up like a two-year-old on Christmas morning.

His best friend had returned. I had more pleasure in giving Maynard that Bible than anything I can ever remember doing.

Maynard continued to grow in the Lord and was faithful to our services. He realized that he had to find a better job because it was difficult to get by on minimum-wage pay. Maynard found work as a carpet layer's apprentice. Because of his hard work and dedication to his employer, the company sent him to another city—with a higher salary—to work for them in a new store they had just opened.

Several months later I had an opportunity to converse with a carpet layer from that city, and I asked him if he knew Maynard. He said, "Yes, I know that _____" (profanity). He continued, "All Maynard talks about is Jesus Christ and that crazy Baptist church he is always trying to get people to go to." I said, "Praise the Lord!" The man just looked at me as if I were as crazy as Maynard. But it thrilled my heart to hear such a glowing testimony from an unbeliever about one of Satan's former slaves, who is now a discipled Christian.

Go ye therefore, and teach all nations, baptizing them in the name of the Father, and of the Son, and of the Holy Ghost: teaching them to observe all things whatsoever I have commanded you: and, lo, I am with you alway, even unto the end of the world. Amen (Matt. 28:19, 20).

Maynard experienced release from Satan's cords of sin. There is hope and escape for a new Christian who has been one of Satan's slaves—if he really wants it. As mature Christians, we often fail to teach new believers the simple truth that sin is not something to be enjoyed but rather something to be hated. When we see sin as being exceedingly sinful and Satan as a brutal taskmaster, we will begin to see greater success in helping free his slaves from their bondage.

CHAPTER TWELVE

A Red-Hot Wedding

Many people are saddled by boredom and the humdrum of life. Having grown up in the hills of West Virginia, I remember a most exciting event—the neighbor's cat gave birth to nine kittens. Many days would pass before "excitement" again rumbled through our abeyant lives.

In contrast, boring inactivity is never the case in our big cities. Among the throbbing sounds we become accustomed to is the shrillness of sirens screaming in the night. Hearing the sirens is the most chilling moment one can experience. They are a reminder that people are continually being scuttled into eternity as though some giant hand were scooping them up with reckless abandon and hurling them out beyond the boundary of compassion and into an endless abyss.

One Saturday afternoon while I was officiating at a wedding, the sirens began to wail. I didn't give them much thought until the fire trucks stopped at our house next door. At about the same time, my wife ran in, interrupting the ceremony in progress and saying, "Our house is going to burn down." We immediately stopped the wedding and rushed outside. The house next to ours was fully enveloped with fire, and the flames lapped under the eaves of the church parsonage. I grabbed our garden hose and began to spray our house, trying to get it wet enough to keep it from catching on fire. As more fire equipment arrived on the scene, the firemen brought the blaze under control, and our house was spared from the fate of the house next door.

The firemen put out the fire, and we returned to conclude the wedding. I realize that there should be a little fire in a marriage, but this wedding turned out to be one hot ceremony!

The house that had stood beside ours had been built in the late 1800s. It was known as "Queen Ann's Mansion" and was a landmark for the near-west side of Cleveland. It had been divided into apartments, and nine people resided there. All the people escaped, but some of their pets perished in the blaze.

The arson division of the fire department determined the fire had been deliberately set, and someone reportedly saw two teens running away from the house when it started to burn. Gasoline had been thrown on the front stairway and lower hall. The boys were never apprehended, and so their motive was never known. Speculations are many. Some say it was peer pressure; others say it was a prerequisite for proving bravery in order to gain membership into one of the area gangs. Still others speculate that the owner paid arsonists to set the building on fire because seven other properties he owned have also been the objects of arsonists.

Whatever the reason, fires happen almost every day in our city. It is not uncommon for more than one home to be burning in our city at the same time. One of our greatest fears is that someone will burn our house down, not because they are mad at us but because they just want to watch it burn. Everyone is searching for some way to prevent these things from happening, but we are scoffed at when we suggest that if more effort were spent in rescuing Satan's slaves, the problem would be solved.

As much as goes on in the city, it seems there is not enough entertainment to keep the slaves amused. One thing people are constantly faced with is the random shooting of guns. Almost every week we discover new bullet holes in the church—gunners simply shoot at it. Presently we had to install bulletproof glass. Also on the steeple of the church sits a metal ball that must present a challenging target. Of course, most of the time the shooters miss and instead rip holes in the roof. We never become overly alarmed because it is so routine. I do not believe these people are trying to harm anyone. The shooting is done for amusement's sake and for excitement.

As we travel from place to place, we discover that there are few differences in any major city. Whether it be Buffalo, Detroit, Philadelphia or Cleveland, all are about the same. Few who live outside the big cities know of the world that exists within them. But here lie mission fields that have suffered from neglect for many years. It is time we truly make an effort to reach them with the same message we are taking overseas.

CHAPTER THIRTEEN

Abused Families

Most teens in the inner city feel that they are street-wise and can take care of themselves. It sometimes becomes very difficult to deal with them. They are under many pressures. They have to contend with parental pressures as well as extreme peer pressure. Yet I believe that peer pressure is easier for them to deal with because they are on the same wave length as the other teens and understand where they are coming from. Parental pressure is quite a different story. Sometimes I think that life in the inner city affects people to the point where they have a difficult time dealing with reality and parenthood. Satan certainly has many slaves among inner-city families.

One of the families I have worked with for many months has helped me understand the situation a little better. There are five children in this particular family. Over the many months, the five children—from eleven to eighteen years of age—have made professions of faith in Christ.

They live in a particularly rough neighborhood, and we have spent many hours counseling and praying with them. I have brought food and put it on the table, as well as put clothes on their backs. My family and I have been faithful in picking them up for church and trying to include them in every activity the church engaged in. One would think that if someone spent this much of their time and money, the parents would show some gratitude. After many months of our working with the family, the mother finally made a profession of faith and was baptized. After she became a member of our church, she attended the services just a few times.

The father is an alcoholic and enjoys beating his family. I have been in the home when he has hit the girls with his fists and knocked them across the room. I have seen them lying on the floor with bloody noses and cut lips. I have observed the mother with cuts over her face and bruises on her body. The end result has had such an effect upon this family that it is hard to describe. Each of the teenage girls has had illegitimate children—some, I suspect, by the father—and they have run away from home repeatedly. These girls are professing Christians; yet they are unable to break the bonds that bind them to the old way of life.

One afternoon I received a long distance phone call—collect, of course—from one of the girls. She did not even know which state she was in. She had run away from home and had begun hitch-hiking. A trucker had picked her up, and she had spent a day or two on the road with him. What does one do for these people? About all one can do is pray for them, counsel with them and try to provide some of the love that the parents should be providing. It doesn't do much good to call the welfare department because many other families are in worse shape than this one, and it is hard to get them to respond.

The father is strongly influenced by his environment. He has no desire to find employment and holds contempt for all government programs. He feels that the government could give him more, if only it would. He holds contempt for anyone who doesn't give him something for nothing. Several years ago while working on a roof, he was slightly hurt and has been on the welfare programs ever since. He feels that a person who works is a sucker. The man has deep emotional problems and is a habitual liar. In fact, he is so adept at lying that he can convince you that what he is saying is the absolute truth.

Many people think that someone can call the welfare department and get help for mistreated and abused children. This idea perhaps comes about because of the few cases where good Christians have been harassed by the welfare department over the proper discipline of their children. Let me share something written by Richard Thomas in a Cleveland newspaper, August 21, 1984: "How Badly Does Welfare Mishandle Abuse Reports? As part of their efforts to change the way the Cuyahoga County Welfare Department deals with reports of child sex abuse, members of the Community Advocates for Sexually Abused Children (CASAC) met with the Welfare Department Director, Marjorie Hall-Ellis, August 17 at the West Side Multi-Service Center."

The following is a testimony given to two CASAC members at the meeting:

A young girl was sexually assaulted numerous times by her stepfather over a period of several months. After each assault, she reported it to the Welfare Department's child abuse hotline, 696-KIDS, but no action was taken. She also ran away after each assault, only to be picked up and returned to her home. Eventually she was sent to a home for juveniles for being incorrigible. The stepfather still lives at home with the girl's sisters.

Employees of a local agency reported a suspected case of sex abuse to the 696-KIDS line as required by law. A follow-up call twelve days later revealed that the case had been lost. Employees described the situation again, and the Welfare Department sent a letter to the parents of the family. The letter stated that the department had received a report about the care of the child and requested that the family come into the office to be interviewed. The first appointment was canceled due to an unexplained emergency. A week went by before the family came in, and during that time the child was still at home with the alleged abuser. When questioned, the child denied being abused. Although the caseworker said she believed that abuse was taking place, she said the case would be closed because there were no legal grounds to proceed further.

The above are just two examples of the many instances of mishandling that CASAC claims to be aware of. Welfare Department officials claim to have a 90 percent success rate in validating sex abuse reports. But CASAC members think otherwise.

"We're not talking about two or three cases, not cases that have fallen through the cracks in the system or happen because of 'worker error,' " said Dan Joyce from the Community Youth Mediation Program (CYMP) at the meeting. "The people in this room have personal knowledge of 60 cases that the Welfare Department has mishandled. Since we represent a limited geographical area, we fear this is just the tip of the iceburg."

The CASAC is a coalition of fifty-one community groups and agencies in Cleveland, most from the near-west side, that was formed to address the "alarming practices and procedures" in handling cases of sex abuse.

When the Welfare Department receives a sex-abuse report and the alleged victim can be contacted only at home, the caseworker attempts to contact the parents either by phone or by letter, inviting the family into the office to be interviewed. Initial contact in the family's home is avoided.

CASAC members charge that this procedure endangers the child; it not only tips off the abuser that he or she has been reported, but it also allows time for the abuser to pressure or coerce the child into denying the abuse. Since it can take a long time to get the family in for an interview and determine what is happening, the child is left vulnerable, they point out.

"I'd like to know how anyone with common sense can believe that sending a letter will not endanger the child," said Charley Burns, a CYMP volunteer.

The members of CYMP began meeting with Andrea Goodloe, supervisor of the Welfare Department unit that investigates sex-abuse reports. CYMP found that there was no written policy governing the investigation process, according to Sue Meyers, a CASAC member and a teacher at Urban Community School.

It is sometimes difficult to become aroused by what one reads in the newspapers, but when a person is involved firsthand and knows that there is nothing he can do to prevent child abuse, he feels helpless. My heart aches to do something about the situation of the family in my church, but I am helpless to interfere. The only hope is for the father to become a Christian, but he is at present extremely negative toward a gospel witness.

Escape and Recapture

As I previously stated, unemployment is a vicious slave owner, and few really know it as the inner-city dweller does. The languor created by this slave owner makes its victims more susceptible to imprisonment. Complacency prohibits liberation. Unemployment conceals the slave owner as he lies in ambush for his victim.

The camouflage was so clever that Don did not even know that he was being stalked until it was too late. He had been employed for several years at the same place. His employer was trying to be fair and keep his employees happy and earn a decent wage himself. However, things deteriorated rapidly because of employee theft.

Something had to be done in order to curb the losses. The boss decided that he would lay off one man at a time until the thief was no longer working. Then he would call back the others. Don was the last one laid off when the losses ceased. The employer immediately called the others back to work.

Now that Don was unemployed, things really became complicated for him. He was a compulsive gambler and liar who was so settled in his sin that he apparently could not distinguish truth from falsehood. He would take his welfare check and gamble it away on the horses and then report that the check had been stolen.

Don's wife didn't consider her marriage vows sacred and often took a lover. She has three children; only two of them were fathered by her husband. She suffers from schizophrenia.

Both Don and Mae have been going to church for many years and have made several professions of faith. Their three children have developed the unstable ways of their parents. The oldest girl has run away several times with different men—the only criteria, the man must have a few dollars and a car. The middle child is very intelligent. He often assists his father in stealing what they can. Usually the father distracts the store owner while his son makes off with merchandise. The youngest son is very unruly and also a thief. We have caught him going through purses in church and also stealing from missionary displays. It was very embarrassing to me when the store owner across the street asked me to please not let these particular members of my church come over to his store on Sunday. He said, "They steal everything that isn't nailed down." He didn't want to have them arrested because it would be an embarrassment to our congregation.

When Mae and her youngest child were in church, one would never know who would disturb the service more. The boy would begin to talk out loud or blow a big bubble with his gum. Mae would raise her voice as though she were outside and tell him to quit it or to shut up.

One Sunday during the invitation, Don came forward with tears of remorse. I decided to deal with him personally, and I turned the service over to a deacon. We went to one of the Sunday School rooms where we could talk freely. He said that he couldn't find a job, and this lack of employment is what had caused so many problems. I asked him if that were the real problem, and he finally admitted his real need was that he had never been saved. He said that the other times he responded to the invitation, he was trying to eliminate guilt. He said that someone would pray with him, but he would soon be back where he had been.

That morning he did all the praying with much tears. I thought we now had a foundation to build upon. After several counseling sessions, I baptized Don and began a discipling program. Several weeks went by, and there seemed to be much improvement in his attitude and conduct. He claimed to have several job prospects and expected to be working in Alabama soon.

One evening he came to me and said that he had bought bus tickets for the entire family, but that someone had stolen his wallet on the way back from the bus terminal. He needed $400 in order to get his family to Alabama so he could go to work on Monday. I made some phone calls and found that he had been to the race track that day and that the place of employment in Alabama did not know him and had not hired him. When I confronted him with this, he began to cry; then he got mad because he said I didn't trust him and had embarrassed him before his family! He said, "A preacher is supposed to help people, not hurt them." From that day, Don has not attended any church services.

Mae sometimes comes, but, again, her attendance always results in disruption of church services. We keep hoping that someday they will truly trust Christ and make Him Lord of their lives. There are times when the flesh begins to take over and we feel like telling them to please stay at home. We know that the children would benefit from a good application of the strap, but that would result only in litigation. Each time they came forward to dedicate their lives to Christ, their "decision" (if you can call it that) was short-lived, and soon they returned to their former ways. I knew this would be the end result each time, but I kept hoping it would be real someday. It seemed that they could escape from their "owner" for only a few short days, and then they were recaptured.

CHAPTER FIFTEEN

Robbery Victim

Crime is rampant throughout our nation, but our cities hold the greatest concentration of criminals. The greater the population, the easier it is to find victims. Those of us familiar with the streets realize that caution must be taken at all times. I wonder if people not familiar with street life even vaguely realize that someone is probably carefully watching them when they visit the big city.

I have observed people removing their wallets or pulling several bills from their pockets in order to purchase something from a street vendor. If you are foolish enough to do this, you are looking for trouble. I have also observed people pulling up close to the car in front of them when stopping at a red light. If you do not leave yourself room to escape in case of trouble, you could be the next victim of a robbery. Locking your doors is good, but locked doors offer little protection from the "smash-and-grab" robber. A brick through your side window is so sudden that you often freeze and are unable to react as someone reaches through the broken window and snatches your valuables from the front seat.

Even if you are wise to the possibilities that exist on the streets, your wisdom is often of little consequence. I thought that I was taking sufficient precautions to avoid being another statistic, but I was mistaken.

One evening just before dark, I needed to go to the bank to make a withdrawal at the automatic teller. I did not take Klipper with me, and I couldn't go before the bank closed for the day. As I approached the bank, I was careful to examine the area. Two men, whom I had not seen hiding behind a cement column, jumped out and stuck a razor knife in my back and demanded my wallet as I was using the automatic teller. I felt that it was more logical to give them my wallet than my blood, so I complied with their wishes. They turned away, but I felt that some resistance was called for since the knife was no longer pressed into my lower back.

I kicked at the one who had my wallet in one hand and the knife in the other. I missed my aim, but I did hit his elbow. The knife went flying and so did he—as fast as he could go into the projects located across the street from the bank. I knew better than to follow him in there because my safety would have been in jeopardy. I grabbed the other man and wrestled him to the ground and tried to keep him from escaping. Next to the bank is one of Cleveland's better known hospitals. There are always security guards on duty there, and this evening was no exception. Two guards had witnessed the whole episode, and I called to them for assistance. They refused because they said that it was against the rules to become involved in anything off the hospital property. I could no longer hold the man I had captured because he was bigger than I was and was struggling violently to get away. He finally ran into the projects as his partner had.

I called the police and made a report of the incident. The next morning I called the bank and had them cancel payment on the checks that were also stolen. They put a stop-payment on my credit cards as well. The bank informed me that it was impossible for the thieves to know the secret number of my instant cash card and that I should not worry about it. I foolishly believed them.

We had taken out an automatic advance loan in case of emergencies, and my account had a one-thousand-dollar automatic advance on it. Any time a system is developed to aid bank customers, the criminals have a way of bypassing the bank security. Apparently some character has a computer that can read the secret number—for a fee, of course. The thieves obtained my number and began to make withdrawals from my account. After my money was exhausted, the bank began to make automatic advances to cover the overdrafts. Not only did the thieves withdraw one thousand dollars, they caused the checks that I had legitimately written to bounce as well. By the time we had bought back the bounced checks, we were out $1800! The thieves also ran up about $500 on the Master Card, but the bank absorbed that. We were advised to get a lawyer and fight the case, but the lawyer advised us to forget it. My wife also had a card, and we had no way of proving that we hadn't taken this opportunity to make the withdrawals ourselves. The bank refused to show any sympathy, even though one of their managers had advised us not to worry about the money card. By the way, she refused to admit that she had said this because it would have cost her her job for giving out such foolish information.

Eventually one man was caught. Evidently he had stolen some-one else's checks and was writing the checks to me and using my identification to cash the checks. He had split my driver's license and inserted one of his pictures in it.

Sometimes you wonder about the system that is supposed to protect a person. This man had had many prior arrests. At the time he robbed me, he was on parole from a sentence of serving five to fifteen years for armed robbery. While he was out on bail for robbing me, he also committed another armed robbery. The robber had spent most of his life behind bars and was, without a doubt, a habitual criminal. Think about it! A parole violator was not returned to the institution but was granted bail. The excuse for letting him out was that the prisons are overcrowded. At first, we were bitter toward the man and the system that permitted him to walk the streets; but as we thought about it, we realized he is just one of Satan's slaves. The system is a vehicle that Satan uses to keep his slaves under control.

Incidents like this cause city dwellers to live in fear and keep themselves behind locked doors. If we are ever going to set men free from the bonds of Satan, we must relinquish the safety of locked doors and venture upon the streets. Incarceration failed to liberate this man from his desire to live his life as a criminal.

Environmental changes, whether social or institutional, can never change the inner man and create the ideal citizen. If a man is to be changed, the change must come from within. A person must have a transformed heart that is the result of the new birth. Only Jesus Christ can effect this transformation. Society knows this, but they refuse to acknowledge it because their whole humanistic philosophy is built upon the lie that man can govern himself without any acknowledgment of an Almighty God. If God thought it was important enough to send His only Son to a sin-filled earth with the truth, shouldn't we think it is important enough to go to the cities of our nation with it?

CHAPTER SIXTEEN

God Calls His Missionaries

Even after reading about life in the inner city, some may ask, How difficult would it be for me to work in an inner-city ministry? The answer to that question will vary with the individual. I feel that it would be a very difficult task were it not that God equips certain people for such a task. I believe that God uses an individual's personality as well as his talents and spiritual gifts. In order to be effective in inner-city work, the individual must have an aggressiveness as well as compassion. I have encountered many pastors who were exceptionally suited for their particular place of service but who would be overwhelmed by the inner city. An individual cannot fool himself into believing that he can adapt to the situation. The discouragements are too numerous and the dangers far too great for the average person.

I do not want to imply that I am something special. I am an individual with a temperament suited for the situation and one whom God saw fit to call for a special assignment. Some have stated about our location that their "guardian angel" would not walk the streets with them if they were here. I have already stated that I happen to believe that the center of God's will is the safest place on earth. Don't ever feel sorry for the missionary. He is unique. He is one who has answered the call of God, and he is happy and contented with his place of service.

The thing that moves my heart so much is that few feel any real burden for the people of the inner city. Christians readily support missions on a foreign field but fail to see any real need here at home.

Another thing that bothers me is that some churches support the mission field but not the individual missionary. By that I mean that they will support whoever is on the particular field that they want represented by their church. Perhaps there is nothing wrong with supporting missions in that way, but I do not believe that it is a wise decision.

Before a church ever considers supporting a man, it should first have good and acceptable confidence in the mission board that he is associated with. If they have fully investigated the board, it will know the missionary has been meticulously screened before he was accepted under its auspices. The church will know the missionary is doctrinally sound and separated from worldly living. If a church invites a missionary who represents a mission board that does not practice sound Biblical doctrine and separation from those who practice unscriptural positions, they are unwise stewards of their time or finances. Many churches find themselves in embarrassing situations because of this practice. If a missionary accepts funds from a church that is associated with unscriptural positions, then he himself is unworthy of God's people and their blessings.

I find in the ministry that there are many men who are called into the ministry by Mom and equipped or educated by Dad. It is sad that this is true. Many churches, in their quest for a pastor, fail to completely seek the mind of God before they call a man. This man will ruin the testimony of the church and fail to lead them properly because he is not called of God and does not seek the mind of God before he makes decisions. I often come into contact with missionaries who are in this category and who are supported by good churches and pastors who have been deceived by them. This type of missionary is lazy and does not have the ambition to do the work of God in a manner that the present hour demands. When a man is called of God and he surrenders to the will of God, everything else must be laid aside for the work whereunto he is called.

I believe that every church has an obligation to spend much

time in prayer before calling a man to be pastor. If churches would do this, there would be fewer "deadbeats" in our churches. I also believe that a church should spend just as much time in prayer before selecting a missionary to support. When a church, after much prayer, decides to have a part in the ministry of a particular missionary, it should stand behind him 100 percent.

Ten dollars a month is not support! If a man is worthy of your support and God has definitely impressed you to support him, then he is worthy of sacrificial giving. Some churches just starting are limited as to what they can do, but they should bring a missionary's support to a respectable amount as the congregation grows and before they consider involving themselves in the ministry of other missionaries. Some churches enjoy boasting about the number of missionaries they support. To say that one supports seventy-five missionaries around the world sounds good. And indeed it is good to support seventy-five missionaries if you are giving them enough to justify the price of the stamp on the envelope!

Almost everywhere we go, we hear people in our churches praying, "Lord, raise up more missionaries." This prayer is commendable, but I also think it is shameful that we have not sent to the field those whom God has already raised up. It takes the average missionary about two years to raise his support and passage for the field! We should turn to Revelation 3:14–19 and ask if Jesus' words could possibly be true of our churches as well.

As we address the question at the beginning of this chapter, we must first realize that inner-city missions is very difficult, and it is impossible to be effective unless you are, first of all, called of God to do the work. When God selects a man for this type of mission work, He will choose a man who has the temperament to withstand the pressures that this ministry will impose upon him. The man of God on the streets must be able to say no, even though every fiber in his body cries out to react to the deplorable situation in certain ways. One cannot be effective in the inner city unless he is stern, but at the same time compassionate, with each individual. The people of the inner city will take all they can get because they have been indoctrinated and conditioned by our welfare system. If you are stern without compassion, your true character will show like a flashing neon light.

It doesn't take long before you are able to spot those who are professional rip-off artists. Being able to discern can come only with experience. There are many people who are in desperate need, and it is impossible for one person to meet all their needs. Even though you may not be able to help a person, he must know that you care about him and would help if you could. Many times you must meet physical needs before you are able to minister to him spiritually.

What type of a man is God looking for to serve Him in the inner city? One who is willing to give himself completely to the ministry without regard for his own well-being. One must be willing literally to burn out for God. If one is not willing to give everything that he has for these desperate people, he is better off not accepting the challenge. A quitter makes it more difficult for the other missionary who is willing to give himself to see people saved.

If you are one whom God is calling, I would place this challenge before you. Find a friend or maybe two who would be willing to give you two hours of their time. (There is safety in numbers.) Drive to one of our large cities and walk the streets for a while. Look into the eyes of the men and women as you pass them, and ask yourself these questions: Lonely souls, do you know that Christ died for you? Do you know that there is hope, that there is something tangible that will not crumble beneath you when you grasp it? Notice their eyes—how they dart from place to place, searching, ever searching for something that seems to be eluding them, and they don't even know what they are looking for. See each bag lady, carrying everything she owns in a paper sack, searching through garbage cans for something of value that someone else threw away. See her eyes light up over a used-up tube of lipstick or perhaps some hose with large runs in them.

The clothes of the street people are ripped, their shoes have holes in them, their stomachs are empty and hurting, and their souls are desperate for the good news that someone really cares for them and loves them. As you look into their forlorn, despairing faces and see the hopelessness that radiates from them and you are moved with the same compassion that Christ was moved with as He looked out over Jerusalem, then you are a candidate for the work of Christ in that place.

You must have a broken heart that is full of compassion and a determination to do what you can. I believe that the best definition that I can give you for compassion is "to hurt for another." If it is not God's will for you to go, then get behind the man whom God has called to go. *He needs your financial support* because he will give to others to the point that he puts his own personal needs in jeopardy. *He needs your prayers* because he will be in constant danger. He will know discouragement to the point that he might quit because he feels that no one really cares and that he is giving his very life and health to a people who don't even seem to care.

I challenge you, the reader, to pray as you never have before for the men and women who are working in our large cities. It is not enough to pray, "God bless all our missionaries. . . ." These men and women need to be remembered by name every day. They need to be reinforced by the knowledge that you are praying for them, by name. This faithfulness will require some effort from you.

You need to write the missionaries a letter to let them know that you and your prayers are behind them. You also might consider sending a little money to them because you know that every day they give money and food to those in desperate need. They deprive their families of some of the luxuries that you take for granted. They are in the cities by themselves with their families. They cannot afford to hire an assistant to help relieve some of the burdens of the ministry.

The inner-city missionaries do not have anyone to answer their telephones, and you wonder why you cannot reach them when you call. They are probably out on the streets or in the home where a tragedy has just occurred. They do not have anyone to clean the small church or write their correspondence while they should be giving themselves to study and prayer in preparation for the next message. They do not have anyone to teach Sunday School for them; therefore, they have to prepare to teach a lesson that will meet the needs of and be understood by children, teens and adults alike. Their lesson cannot be too simple or too complex.

Yes, your missionaries to the lonely, forgotten people of the inner city are unique. They have answered God's call and are willing to give everything in order to be obedient to their Master. They are not in the large city in order to gain some favor or to use their records as stepping-stones for future ministry. They are there as servants to the people for whom Christ died.

And a vision appeared to Paul in the night; there stood a man of Macedonia, and prayed him, saying, Come over into Macedonia, and help us. After he had seen the vision, immediately we endeavoured to go into Macedonia, assuredly gathering that the Lord had called us for to preach the gospel unto them (Acts 16:9, 10).

For whosoever shall call upon the name of the Lord shall be saved.

How then shall they call on him in whom they have not believed? and how shall they believe in him of whom they have not heard? and how shall they hear without a preacher? (Romans 10:13, 14).

Come with David Dolin and witness the world of the inner city—crime, poverty and despair. Be introduced to drug dealers, prostitutes, victims of Satan worship, drug users, abused families, gang members and religious devotees—all Satan's slaves in the inner city. Cry and rejoice with Dolin as he tells of the struggles, defeats and victories of working among those people to emancipate them from Satan's bonds. Dare to develop a burden for the needy people of the inner city and those who minister to them.

David Dolin is a missionary with Baptist Mid-Missions. He and his wife served for five years in an inner-city ministry in Cleveland and for two years in Alaska. They are now serving in Nova Scotia, Canada.

RBP

RBP5159   ISBN 0-87227-129-3